THE BEST OF

2002

D1469545

'It might itch a bit –
we've hidden an
NHS waiting list inside'

MATTHEW PRITCHETT studied at St Martin's School of Art in London and first saw himself published in the *New Statesman* during one of its rare lapses from high seriousness. He has been the *Daily Telegraph*'s front-page pocket cartoonist since 1988. In 1995, 1996 and 1999 he was the winner of the Cartoon Arts Trust Award and in 1991 he was 'What the Papers Say' Cartoonist of the Year. In 1996, 1998 and 2000 he was *UK Press Gazette* Cartoonist of the Year and in 2002 he received an MBE.

The Daily Telegraph

THE BEST OF

2002

'Hello, my cat is stuck up a tree, could someone clone another one for me?'

ORION

Orion Books
A division of the Orion Publishing Group Ltd
Orion House
5 Upper St Martin's Lane
London WC2H 9EA

First published by Orion Books in 2002

A CIP catalogue record for this book
is available from the British Library

ISBN 0 75284 921 2

Printed and bound in Great Britain by
Butler & Tanner Ltd, Frome and London

THE BEST OF

'It's a new breed of
non-working dog'

Law and Order

'That doesn't look like a house...
you're nicked!'

'Are you Spot?'

Law and Order

'Is this your first time in solitary confinement?'

'When do we get to trash a McDonald's, Sarge?'

Law and Order

'CHILL OUT! It's the police'

'Would you let me off the speeding ticket if I said I was on my way to buy some ecstasy?'

Law and Order

'I've suffered far less vehicle related crime lately – my car was stolen six months ago'

'Tidy the place up! I've invited my boss back for dinner'

The Armed Forces

The War on Terror

'Ooops . . . I was just looking for my Christmas presents'

'Have you met Colonel Wilson, our local warlord?'

The War on Terror

'And another thing, Osama –
you never take us anywhere'

'I was just thinking, Osama,
you love death and I would
love $25 million . . .'

Reward offered for Osama

The War on Terror

'This won't be over quickly–
it could take years'

'We'll show the terrorists that
they can't stop our recession'

The War on Terror

'I'm happy to fetch your paper, but I draw the line at opening your post'

'What if it's full of anthrax?'

The War on Terror

'Is that your new aftershave or has there been a chemical warfare attack?'

'Had they sold out of gas masks?'

The War on Terror

'The credit card is fine, but your signature reveals that you're a fanatical lunatic bent on world destruction'

The War on Terror

'We want to go to a country
that hasn't upset
President Bush'

'Just because he didn't return
your ladder doesn't mean
you can call him part of
an axis of evil'

The War on Terror

'I've forgotten whether I'm
a military expert or an
economics expert'

'Sir, can you halt the war for a
while? My arm's getting tired'

The War on Terror

'I'm into my sixth day of not being too bothered about the al-Qa'eda prisoners'

'If that's my wife, tell her my itinerary is being kept secret for security reasons'

Airline slump

'There was a near miss yesterday. Two passengers came within 100ft of each other'

'I'm going to the loo to have a cigarette'

Country Life

Hunting banned – but
gambling gets go-ahead

'I suppose self-regulation
is out of the question?'

Country Life

Hunting banned in Scotland

'We believe the fox is hiding somewhere near this network of dens'

Transport – and Byers

'European railways are terrible –
if you show up at the station
just ten minutes late the
train has already gone'

Transport – and Byers

'The timetable isn't misleading, it's just based on unfortunate misunderstandings'

'Are you trying to bury some bad news about the 7.15?'

Transport – and Byers

'If anyone complains about the
7.15, try to smear their family'

'When I started this
journey, Stephen Byers
was still a rising star'

Transport – and Byers

'It's a sweepstake on the
date Byers will be sacked'

'It's what he would
have wanted'

... and finally he goes

The World of Science

'You think you've got problems, I've started laying fried eggs'

'Ladies and gentlemen, we're very close to creating the ideal human being'

The World of Science

'You're about to feel the stress just melting away'

Asylum

'An asylum centre? I was hoping it was a post office'

'I'm willing to work during England's World Cup matches'

Asylum

'He would look angrier,
but he's had the Boots
Botox injection'

'Repeat after me,
"I have been carjacked"'

Asylum

'I just hope they make an effort
to fit in with our culture'

Refugee ship heads
for Australia

The Church

'I don't want to incite religious hatred, vicar, but that's your third slice of cake'

'It's Easter, Vicar, why aren't you at the garden centre?'

Archer

'Lord Archer is claiming to be at a better prison than is actually the case'

'That's the last time I visit Jeffrey; there wasn't even a glass of Krug on offer'

The Nation's Health

'Put it this way, we're looking at an extra 2p on tax just for you'

'I'd like someone else to have my tax bill'

There's no such thing as a free operation

The Nation's Health

'Don't worry, you'll forget about the pain in your knee when you see your next tax bill'

'It's from the Inland Revenue'

The Nation's Health

'I've come to visit
my money'

'Take a seat, and within
20 minutes you will be seen
by a tax inspector'

The Nation's Health

'And here's one of me in Lille'

'Now, about your operation in France. Could you bring us back 200 cigarettes and a few bottles of Cognac?'

Patients farmed out

The Nation's Health

'Good news, the Taliban are surrendering Kandahar. You'll be going there for your hip operation soon'

'The treatment didn't work, your body has rejected private medicine'

The Nation's Health

'We've scrapped the waiting list. You're now on the NHS ten year plan'

'You have what we in the medical profession call "a heck of a long wait"'

The Nation's Health

'This should make the waiting list seem shorter'

'My business has taken over this hospital and I'm afraid I'm going to have to let you go'

The Nation's Health

'I'm afraid your appendix has become a political football'

'I've been here eight hours and I still haven't been mentioned in the House of Commons'

The politics of health

The MMR Debate

'And here's a lollipop
for being so brave'

'It's love, passion and devotion –
we give the three jabs
together nowadays'

Air Traffic Control ...

Teething problems...

... And Plane Spotters

'*Actually, I thought I might go
and photograph some other
Greek prisons*'

... And Plane Spotters

'I'm not a spy – I only asked
what was in the taramasalata'

'You have a suspiciously large
number of Acropolis postcards'

The Royals

'I'm attempting to combine the two roles of not working and not being a royal'

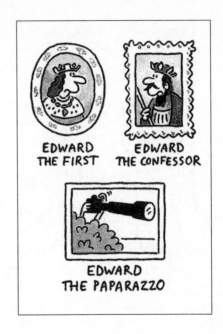

Working Royals

The Royals

'I'm sure this potato salad was left over from the Silver Jubilee'

The Postal Service

'We can use Consignia or a
private mail company'

'I'm using a private mail
company to post myself to work'

Education

'It's much harder to fail exams than it was in your day'

'Let's end these bitter recriminations and look to the future'

Education

'You're an idiot. Discuss'

'Shall we wake him and tell him to stop worrying?'

May Day Riots

'Since last year's demo my flat
has gone up £25,000'

A Question of Politics

'From up here you can see five
different layers of government'

'We're planning to create a
whole new tier of voter apathy'

A Question of Politics

Monkey for Mayor...

...and Le Pen's election campaign

A Question of Politics

'What bad luck; Tony Blair is having terrible weather for his visit to Britain'

'I'm sick of domestic issues – maybe I'd do better on the world stage'

A Question of Politics

'My family have known the
Blairs for years, so I'm a
hereditary crony'

'Jenkins, go out and
kiss some babies for me'

A Question of Politics

'He's always been a Labour
Party man'

'Every day an area the
size of John Prescott
disappears for ever'

Dodgy donations...   ...and freebies

Financial Irregularities

'Gentlemen, the company has undergone some changes since our last board meeting'

'Not even photocopying my bottom would cheer me up today'

Financial Irregularities

'... so, if Johnny has minus 20 billion apples...'

'You see your pension fund as half empty, but I see it as half full'

The World Cup

'It's the World Cup in two
weeks, I'm practising
calling in sick'

'A bowl of cornflakes and have
one yourself'

The World Cup

'Not many of our players are fit enough to walk out'

'...and this little piggy played against Sweden in the World Cup'

The World Cup

'I went berserk and knocked
over the bonsai tree'

The World Cup

'Could I have the day off
tomorrow to watch the match?'

'The World Cup makes them
terribly nervous – it's best to
keep them locked out'

The World Cup

'I'm afraid he's in
a meeting'

'I'm cautioning you for failure
to display an England flag'

The World Cup

'You're never more than eight feet from someone who thinks he's a soccer expert'

'I can't find the lucky underpants I wore for the England v Denmark match'

The World Cup

'Come on, gentlemen, haven't you got offices to go to?'

'You're a heartless employer for giving me time off to watch England v Brazil'

And Wimbledon

'I've just come out of a
difficult World Cup and I
don't want to be hurt again'

'The strawberries were too
expensive so I got us some
crack cocaine instead'

And Finally...

'It was either watch this or go
out and vote'

And Finally . . .

'I wish I had gay parents'

'GAY? I suppose that means I'll have to pay for your wedding!'

Anti-prejudice laws

And Finally . . .

'We have reason to believe you have a child that hasn't been taken to the Harry Potter film'

'Now wasn't that more fun than going to the Harry Potter film?'

And Finally . . .

Bush chokes on snack

And Finally . . .

'I'm trying to finish in less time
than it takes for
property prices to double'

'The previous owners took all
the fixtures and fittings'

And Finally . . .

'Most of what I need to know is stored on your ID card'

Invasion of privacy

And Finally . . .

'Can Jimmy come out
to play football?'

'Nobody understands me...shut
up...I hate you...I'm going out'

And Finally . . .

'I'm arresting you for driving in miles instead of kilometres'

And Finally . . .

And Finally . . .

'This hurts me more
than it hurts you, Dad'

'I've hidden the
TV remote control'

And Finally . . .

And Finally . . .

'Your face doesn't look familiar. Are you a shadow cabinet minister?'

And Finally . . .

'I'd like to have my house valued again, it's been three days since it was last done'

'It'll be 110 years before we have this much fun again'